THE SEED-BOX LANTERN

# The Seed-box Lantern

NEW & SELECTED POEMS

## Diana Hendry

MARISCAT PRESS 2013

Poems © Diana Hendry 2013

ISBN 978 0 946588 67 1

*Acknowledgements*

The Selected Poems are taken from *Making Blue* (Peterloo Poets, 1995), *Borderers* (Peterloo Poets, 2001), *Twelve Lilts: Psalms & Responses* (Mariscat Press, 2003), *Sparks!* (Mariscat Press, 2005; with Tom Pow), *Late Love & Other Whodunnits* (Peterloo Poets/ Mariscat Press, 2008).

Among the New Poems, thanks are due to the editors of the following magazines and anthologies: *Ambit* 206 for 'Cousins', *The Spectator* for 'Falling out of Love with Bookshops', *New Writing Scotland* 26 for 'Other Mothers', *DIN* 1 for 'Father's Doors' (this poem was runner up in the Edwin Morgan International Poetry Competition 2009), *The Edinburgh Review* for 'The Greenhouse', 'Abigail's Garden' and 'The Romantic Couple'.

My love and thanks to my poetry-loving kith and kin: my beloved editor Hamish Whyte, my daughter Kate, my son Hamish, Robyn Marsack, Stewart and Judy Conn, Tom Pow, Rosie Bailey, Gerry Cambridge, Sarah Lefanu, Vivian French, Christine De Luca and Ian McDonough.

—DH

Cover image: detail of 'Poppy Seed Pods', © Sue Vize. Used with kind permission of the artist.

Designed and typeset by Gerry Cambridge
gerry.cambridge@btinternet.com
in LTC Goudy Modern and Carter Sans

Printed by Clydeside Press, 37 High Street,
Glasgow G1 1LX
clydesidepress@btconnect.com

Published by Mariscat Press, 10 Bell Place,
Edinburgh EH3 5HT
hamish.whyte@btinternet.com
www.mariscatpress.com

CONTENTS

From: *Making Blue* | 1995

Making Blue / 11
The Arkadi Ferry / 13
Song for the Sea of Crete / 14
Artemis, Still Hunting / 16
Sunbathing Song / 17
Piano Lessons / 18
In Defence of Pianos / 19
Solo / 21
Our Grendel / 22
Soliloquy to a Belly / 23
The Stranger / 25
Dressing Mother / 27


From: *Borderers* | 2001

The Borderers / 31
Demon Lover / 32
The Real and Unreal Scot / 33
The Children's Tale / 34
Seals / 35
The Lost Memories of Llamas / 36
Lowry's House / 38
Apple Sense / 39
Waiting / 40
My Father's Chandelier / 41
International Trader / 42
Drinking Brandy on Whitstable Beach / 43
Arkadi Monastery / 44

From: *Twelve Lilts: Psalms & Responses* | 2003

Psalm 84 / 49
Longing / 51
Psalm 88 Blues / 52
Psalm 90 / 53
Sparrow Song / 54
Psalm 102 / 55
Call / 56
A Low Lilt / 57
Psalm 150 / 58
The Drummer / 59


From: *Sparks!* | 2005

A Guide takes Henri Rousseau on a Tour ... / 63
Glenogle Swim Centre / 64
Two Rounds / 65
To an Unborn Grandchild / 66


From: *Late Love & Other Whodunnits* | 2008

Reading in Bed / 69
Why it Took So Long / 70
Application / 71
Fall-out / 72
About Your New Family / 73
Big Sister's Coming on a Visit / 74
Astanga Poetry / 75
At Miss Foulkes Secretarial College / 76
Seven Blessings / 77
Last Post / 78

To W. S. Graham / 79
Harbours / 80

*New Poems*

How to Play the Piano / 83
Other Mothers / 85
Father's Doors / 86
Cousins / 87
The Warning / 89
Wind, Go Easy / 90
Economy McConomy / 91
Cargo / 92
In Praise of the Variscan / 94
Lament for my Spiral-bound Reporter's Notebook / 95
Caroline Herschel: Her CV / 96
The Romantic Couple: A Fantasy / 97
Lighting Effects / 98
On Falling Out of Love with Bookshops / 99
Dear Miss Armstrong / 100
The Greenhouse / 102
November on Campus / 103
A Street Incident / 104
An English Woman Eats a Vegetarian Haggis / 105
Yellow Poppies / 106
Abigail's Garden / 107
Jacob and the Angel / 108
The Visit / 109
In the Swim / 110
The Cure / 111
Kaddish / 112

*For Anne & Henry
with love*

From: *Making Blue* | 1995

## Making Blue

Here, in the harbour, the water is green.
Small fish needle themselves in and out
of its sheen, changing colour like wives
anxious to please a capricious spouse. Was
it fish taught the women how to embroider,
sitting, in black, in their doorways and dark
interiors, needles a tiny, fishy dash?

The nets of the fishermen are ochre and
bobbled with fat pink radishes. Picked
clean (by fingers stubborn as birds beaking
out worms) and spread on deck, here's a flash
jewelled cloak for the Merman King. How he'd
trail and boast it over his shoulder! How
richly the ruby radishes gleam! A giant's

baked sand-pies of concrete then tumbled
them out of his sack to fatten the quay.
The lighthouse, repro Venetian, explicitly
phallic, corkscrews its reflection back to
a notion someone once had concerning spirals.
Under the lighthouse, on its big stone doorstep,
a party of brightly-coloured tourists move

like cells on a microscope plate, afloat
in a fluid of sea and sky. Look—now
there's joining, now dividing. Over the water
you can hear them laughing, not knowing
what moves them, believing it's all their own
volition that pulls them into a cluster,
makes a trio, resolves it all in a final

couple, alone and hugging. The sea's trying
to find the far edge of sky. It's out there
somewhere, a roller towel with sea on one side,
sky on the other. When the sea has it measured
they'll go on their round together and
sky look up and sea look down. Till then
there's nothing else to do—except make blue.

# The Arkadi Ferry

Four times a week, regularly, at the same hour,
it sails for Athens. How, when it boasts its departure
with three loud hoots, our spirits, even in sleep,
swell on the crest of it, are drawn as far after
as Antony by the fleet of Cleopatra's glances.
And even if you know all there is to know
of engineering and navigation, it is still miraculous,
such weight and bulk light on the water, its funnels
crouched like two black eagles, its mast a crucifix
held out before it. Pilot and tug boat scuttle
about it like miniature bridesmaids arranging
the waves and the winds. You think that the anchor
will never let go and when, at last, it goes grandly by
the harbour's eye, you want to applaud.

Four times a week, regularly, at the same hour,
it comes back like morning itself or the mother
whose faithful return you childishly doubted.
Is it the knowledge that one day she won't—or can't—
that gives to her arrival the profound relief
of the heart? And when she leaves again, is it
that you know she must, that it's life's imperative
and that for those we love we can only watch
and hope, standing on the quay and waving like mad,
dumbing the words that choke the throat? Over and
over it carries on, the journey out, the coming back
and the silliness of wanting it all to stop,
to be still, to stay forever and ever, though if
it did, we know we'd not know love at all.

# Song for the Sea of Crete

—for Anne and Henry Kernighan

*We are immersed in an enormous song and we shine like humble pebbles as long as they remain immersed in the sea.*
—Kazantzakis

What matters is the sea—its saga
of light and wind and how it is faring
in its marriage with sky. Tonight
sky's drawn the line—will have nothing
to do with sea's incessant desire
to merge in a mist of dusky bliss. Sea
can stay outside and cool its heels.

What matters is the sea and how its master,
the sun, is treating it—beating its morning
metal until all the sparks fly, smelting it
into dimples and dazzles then nightly leaving it
solvent, soldered, sullen, steel.

What matters is the sea—how it hurriedly
flings down a rustle of satin it's forgotten
to iron; its sudden, revelatory blue
as you cut through a mountain
and it's down there heaving in its workshop
of passion, all frantic kerfuffle
and action, shaping waves in crescendos,
honing a cut-throat phrase on a rock.

What matters is the sea: the ECT shock
and blue flash of its voltage; its hurl at land—
a child's leap at its father—its billionth
dash; its rush in and out as for something
that's lost and of urgent importance.

What matters is the sea and the blue-
shadowed duvet it fluffs under the feet
of the tourist Icarus who float-flies over it
on a boat-drawn parachute. What matters
is sea's steady continuum beneath the beach bar's
fatal beat and the way when night at last rides off—
a girl in evening dress on the back of his *Vespa*—
sea just laps it all over as if nothing had happened.

What matters is the sea in the lull
of its harbour waters; its stormy tough stuff
beyond the quay; its beach fandango
in a can-can of petticoats. Mountains matter,
but only to say what the sea isn't.

What matters is the sea; its hunger
and hanker and danger; its hug and exposure;
its dedication to permanent change; its unpluggable
nature; what matters is the sea, the mass
and hugely blessed blue of it; its untranslatable
garbled message and the way it goes sailing out
to forever and ever and takes your heart with it.
What matters is the never-get-to-the-end-of-it sea

in its inky blacks and terrible deeps and how we,
like the lights on the fishermen's boats,
dance on the back of it, live on the edge of it,
breathe and dream and make up songs for it.
The sea. *Thalassa. Thalassa. Thalassa.*

## Artemis, Still Hunting

From the back, promising. Hair: dark, curly (neither
too wild nor too tame and with endearing tendril centre
nape); froth of beard (Virile? Cheery?); specs; shapely
profile, shapelier knee. Colour sense is easy on the eye—
T-shirt an understated grey and shorts (well cut), dark blue.
Alone, a smoker and, god love us, reading a book! He has
the kind of cough it could be nice to wake to in the middle

of the night. I make all 'hello' noises known to man—
glass-clonk, lighter-click, unignorable see-how-much-we
have-in-common flutter of pages. Arrow-twang. Cough.
Nothing. The young Swiss boy, working at the baker's,
(starts at four a.m.) stops on his early way to bed
to chat about his day. The Greek at the table next
to mine asks what I'm reading. 'Po-et-ry', I say

spreading it out like 'Open Sesame'. What does it take
to turn a man's head? If a man hath all manner of promising
thing and shapely knee and hath not curiosity, he is
a soundless symbol. Curiosity takes me down to the corner
kiosk for a bottle of water, the saunter back contrived
to offer Chance the chance of a little soul-matery
or at least an up-front semiotic of another lone,

book-reading Being, wearing, I now see, my all-tame
bedroom slippers. Not that it matters. Heart-throb's
head down, hung-over, heart-broken—or both—over beer.
And anyway, the writing on his T-shirt's clear. 'Sprite',
it says. Just that. Ye gods, how was I to know?
He has a mortal cough. Drinks Amstel. Reads.

# Sunbathing Song
—to the tune of 'All of You'

I hate the sweat of it,
the grease of it,
the turning
as on a barbecue spit of it;
the roast, bake, fry and all the
peel of it;
the white-little-watch-strap-line and toasted
tits of it.

I hate the oil of it,
the boil of it,
the lying
flat on your back for hours and hours of it;
the sexless strip and the stingy dip you
mix with it;
the nine-to-five and the kiss-me-quix
you wear for it.

I hate the glare of it,
the bare of it,
the pubic
waxing bikinis need for it;
the sun when it's high in the sky
doesn't turn me on one bit;
I'd sooner siesta with Kosta in quest of
the hots of it.

I hate the melt of it,
the burnt pelt of it,
the sandy arse
and all the farce of it;
so leave this shady lady
laid in the shade,
baby,
for I love all of it.

## *Piano Lessons*

The terraced rows closed in and crushed you
in their jaws. At number ten, Miss Mildred
in her best front parlour, taught piano
on a neutered upright. All round
the walls were photographs of pupils who
had made the grade—past heroes of the
pianoforte, all capped and gowned and gone.
I found more promise in the piano's gold
and tabooed feet than in those haloed heads.

Somehow Miss Mildred smuggled in Beethoven,
fierce as sailor's rum. Quite drunk
on that illicit stuff, I'd pay my half-
a-crown and sidle from her spinster's den,
prepared to find the neighbours risen
in outrage from their mothy beds.

## In Defence of Pianos

—for Ben Kernighan

In every alien place you find a piano—
schools, hospitals, prisons, asylums,
the homes of friends, your own front room.
Either they have been there forever
with a squeaky pedal and a dud B flat
or they breach-birth a window
and can't get back.

They should be extinct, these stranded uprights
lost in an iron-mongery moonlight
of genteel dust. The grand ones, got up
like mermaids in ebony velvet, bare
the awful symmetry of their jaws
in crocodile smiles
across the Albert Hall.

My Gros and Kallman, Berlin hausfrau, importantly
panelled and touched-up with brass, has two
timing pendulums engraved on her heart.
Her dreaming feet never touch the floor
and despite her homely Song-Book looks
she'll still flannel her hammers
with Wolfgang or Joseph.

O my frog-prince of furniture, I write
in your defence, having heard it said
that the lion's roar matches the desert,
the elephant's blare breaks through the dark,
the bear can snarl at winter and snow
but man has only
a rented piano—

It is not widely known how far through the dark
of a night a piano can go, nor how
it can take to the streets in summer flight
so that hearing it ragging the silence you'd think
that man rented a forest to make a piano,
its falling pine needles
notes from home.

## *Solo*

It's her music that I'll miss—
it's come to be her perfume in the house,
Rachmaninov's Second gate-crashing down the stairs
from the hi-fi gods of appassionata who live in her attic,
Brahms' First high romance and Elgar's cello
scraping the pelvic floor of grief.

She winters on the upright in the basement,
acquiring Mozart and Scarlatti
like a trainee sibyl, parsing rhythms
until the pitiless metronome gives in
to *The Rustle of Spring*. Then the cat runs
and *The Seasons* begin on the violin.

One summer it was all *The Moonlight*,
Christmas, Mozart's *Requiem*. On the journey
back from the Midlands, she lifted the roof off
the mini with hymns—'O still small voice of calm'
sung indiscreetly loud. Hers was the alto part
in the choir. Queer intervals

From Poulenc's *Gloria* came from the bath,
senseless to us, until on the night
it all came clear, as might, perhaps
the seasons of our lives, the full score
of us, heard from afar. Not
the still sad music Wordsworth knew
but more of Mozart in it, and violins
scaring the shadows.

And then I fear false comfort—
but not as much
as the still small voice
and the silence filling up.

## Our Grendel

There must have been something else but sea.
I try to remember the school, the church, the people

but the sea was the real professional—the rest
an amateur production. However vast the cast

the sea went one better, put on an epic,
a clincher. No need to go and check its

credentials. Trading under a host of disguises
the parent company was easily recognised.

The council built a groyne, a wall, iron-railed
and then, in autumn, all else failing

sent for the sandbags. We lived, I suppose,
as the Geats with Grendel, our sandy homes

full of Chinese chests and shrunken skulls,
restless with women and empty of sons.

Grandfathers outside the pub with salt white hair
sat on in uniform and stared out there.

# Soliloquy to a Belly

I have grown a belly.
It has swallowed up
my legs and arms
even my head.

The government owns it.
Their man
comes to examine it
regularly,
like the meter.
I say 'I am behind it,'
but he has his union,
he has his schedule.

The old mothers
have come to my bedroom
to keep their vigil.
They sit and knit
straitjackets for daughters.
It's the species that matters,
it's all quite natural;
little husk,
you're for corn.

Along the street
the no-bellies walk.
In the space between
their breasts and legs
they've a squeeze
of desire, like picnic salt
in a twist of paper.
They'd like a belly to sleep behind.

I'm afraid
my arms and legs
won't grow again.
It happens every day of the week,
you're not unique,
not even special.

I'll hem my sheets,
I'll let them read the meter twice,
I'll be nice to the midwife,
push when I'm told.
I'm lying in
behind this belly,
thin and cold.

# The Stranger

i

I help the midwife make the bed, a sheet
Of plastic first, to keep the mattress clean,
And then the draw-sheet, folded twice. I void
The thought of beds they dig by spade and fix
My mind on how to count the gaps between
The pains and when to push but still do not
Expect this gale force ten and you. Your head's
A bulb that's breaking through the self of me.

I see you crooked within your father's arm
As in a nest. One day I'll love you more
Than I can guess. Right now, resentful, tired,
Undone, I love and hate you all in one,
Reclaim myself and watch you from afar
And wonder—wonder who on earth you are.

ii

We quarrel while you're in the bath. I slap
Your face. You rise, an angry Venus from
The tub. My specs fly off, my hat is drowned.
I flash-back to that bath-time game when I
Played postman, you the giggling parcel bounced
Upon the postman's knees to Mrs Brown's.
(I played her, too). You lived out former lives
As apple, rose and lamb until un-towelled,

Re-born as you. Oh such a carry-on as you
Worked through the rites of growing up. Today
I've trespassed and you've fled. I find a fall
Of undies on the floor like early selves
You've left. I bundle up your childhood years.
Out of their shell you step in self's new gear.

iii

I left you in your student room. You clutched
Old ted, lost all your teenage bluff and looked
Like ten again. The canny cabbie hired
To take me off, was well acquainted with
The autumn trade in freshly grieving Mums.
He had a spiel, Glaswegian, rough upon
My English ear, but though I missed a deal
Of what he said, he rolled his Rs about
Me like a rug and I took comfort from
His theory that the heart breaks only once

And breaking, breaks us in. But now I think
We're always leaving home and that the heart
Is slowly broken open all life through
By love or loss—as mine, by missing you.


iv

At least five times today we've almost met—
This morning in the shop; at a cafe down
The docks; your back disappearing round the block.
I saw your indicator flash its morse
Farewell and then we almost met again
As smiling you ran up to greet someone
Behind me in our street. It seems you're not
The only girl in the world to look like you,
Though each who isn't makes me queasy, scared

That should you suddenly appear I might
Not know you. Queer, but I'm glad of ghosts and fear
That if they leave, I'll lose your shade to pin
Love to. Then love, that hall-light left all night
For you, might break its filament, or fuse.

# Dressing Mother

I help roll her stockings over her feet,
then up to her knees. She's managed her dress
but I free her fingers from the sleeves.
Before the mirror she rouges her cheeks,
combs her thin curls, hands me a bow.
It's scarlet and goes on a ribbon I thread
under her collar and fix with a hook.
Over an hour to dress her today.

Such an innocence stays at the nape of the neck
it fumbles my fingers. I see her binding
bands of scarlet at the ends of my plaits
and fastening the buttons at my back.
Now look—she's dressed as a child off
to some party. I straighten her scarlet bow

and don't want her to go,
don't want her to go.

From: *Borderers* | 2001

## The Borderers

They take their time. Linger, on the border,
like women who go weeks beyond full term
or those who climb to the top of the cliff
then hesitate. What keeps them?
What holds them back? A tough
and worldly umbilical cord perhaps or
maybe the delay's at the other end
and they're caught in an out-patients queue
their names not called.

Relations wait, wipe spittle,
read the paper, pat a pillow,
hold an aloof hand, take tea

and grief, while they, the borderers,
cling on. Is what looks like dreaming
a final drama? Are they back
in childhood's summer? Do they struggle
with demons? Are they being shriven
by an advance party of angels?

It's like that moment when,
seeing off friends at the airport,
you're allowed no further. We wait

for the end, for the gentle finishing touch.
I'd like to think it's a rush of love to the brain,
then out. But when it's over, dream done,
breath drawn, it's us who're left in the dark.

## Demon Lover

Not until someone tells you
he fancies you, do you see
that he's deadly attractive
and wildly promiscuous.
Very soon you're obsessed,
your life not your own,
always wondering when,
he'll seed, spread, touch bone.
You have therapy for infatuation,
the treatment makes you worse.
You try cutting him out of your life
but the cutting hurts. Poison
doesn't work. On some nights
you're wholly in his thrall.
He leaves you, of course—
and for days, weeks, months,
you begin to feel normal.

Then he's back, with that smile,
that dancer's way of metastazing
about your body—almost tenderly.
'I want you, I want you,' he moans,
and you can't resist. Somehow
you made him. Now you're his.

# The Real and Unreal Scot

The invisible man
who parks his car
outside my house every night
is a Real Scot.
It says so on his windscreen
and I believe it.
Often I lie in bed at night
imagining what a Real Scot
looks like.

His eyebrows are heavy
with generations.
His jaw is cleft
from the Stone of Scone.
Porridge and oatcakes
is his complexion.
His balls are the size
of Safeway haggis.
His hair is heather.
His kilt is tartan Swagger.
His bagpipes Wind and Lament.
His legs could leap the Cuillins,
take Princes Street in a single stride.

So huge is he
he'd have to fold himself in five
to squeeze inside
his grubby wee Metro.

Meanwhile
I've grown a tender spot
for the wry and subtle
unreal Scot.

# The Children's Tale

On his treacherous, miles-long journey
from the sewer to the plug-hole
of Mrs Taylor, the class teacher's bath,
Sid the spider has a very hard time.
A rat nearly eats him. A gang
of cockroaches attack him. Narrowly
he escapes drowning under an avalanche
of water by hanging on a thread. Attempting
a wire trapeze he loses a leg. A passing
beetle mocks him. Bravely he labours on
in the dark and the wet and the stench.
The pipe to the plug-hole is steep
as the peak of Kilimanjaro. And just
as he crawls wearily up into the slippery,
icy whiteness of the bath, someone
turns on the shower. The visiting writer
has to rescue Sid, inventing a towel
flung over the side of the bath
so that Sid can clamber, seven-legged,
to safety, spin a nice warm web
in a nice warm corner of the linen cupboard.
Obligingly the children acquiesce
in the story that it is *they* who want
a happily-ever-after ending.

They start a new story about a snail
crunched, crushed and squelched
to slime by the lawn mower monster.

## *Seals*

Someone has stitched them up
in sleeping bags of stained grey satin.

They have a knowledge of legs
as we have of wings.

The clay of them's still soft. Slumbering
on the rocks, trying to harden into rock,

they're haunted either by a time
before they were fastened inside themselves

or by a time to come when their satiny pods
will pop and split and out they'll step

themselves, at last.

# *The Lost Memories of Llamas*

They are making a bridge of rope
across a river in Machu Picchu.
Whether they are doing so
because there is a need for a bridge
or because an American anthropologist
wants to see how the Incas did it,
or for a television programme, isn't clear.
But at any rate, they are getting paid for it
and they come from their villages
in their lovely Peruvian hats,
arms braceleted in loops and coils
of stringy plaited reeds which are bound
into ropes, which are slung over the river,
which a team of men, laughing and joking,
haul, tug taut, and finally anchor.

It takes three days. The chief rigger,
(once a tightrope walker of distinction)
says it's a work of art and when the camera
draws back to show us the swoop of it—
this cat's cradle hung between mountains,
muscular, whiskery and wondrously patterned—
we see that it is. And that the beauty of the bridge
is not in its strength and steadiness but—as in all
attempts at connection—in its risk and sway.

The American anthropologist teeters nervously
across it. (She is wearing a not-so-lovely hat
and smiling a smile of terror.) 'I daren't
look down!' she cries. We want her to look down.
We want her to believe. In art. In the Incas.
In the connections. The llamas have lost
their memory. They take one look and stall.

The last shot shows four men crossing a bridge
in Machu Picchu and, in the reflection of the river,
a shadow bridge and four ancestral shadows crossing.

# Lowry's House

*It's too big you know—I mean life, sir.*
                              —L. S. Lowry


Bleak. That's what everyone called it,
the stone house in Mottram-in-Longdendale,
the very name of the place having the chill
of rigor mortis. Inside, small dark rooms,
fourteen clocks all telling a different time,
portraits of the parents, Rossetti's girls,
a studio at the back, no carpet on the stairs,
no number on the 'phone. 'Cold as a monk's cell'
the rooms upstairs and the hall where at the end
he fell. Outside, a garden never entered,
waist high with weeds and grass.

Could we, to comfort ourselves, pretend
his true home was the Manchester streets,
Salford College of Art, the Easter Fair
at Daisy Nook and not this stone retreat,
the company of clocks, awful thoughts,
the missing of mother, oils? No, *this*
was home, the drab bleak house of art,
where he never meant to stay, then found
he couldn't leave; where no-one
really lives, though the canvases persist
in telling us how vibrantly we did.

# Apple Sense

To live with an apple tree
in your garden is not
to understand it. Today,
for example, it stands
on one leg, answers
February's ice with a snarl
of black spikes. In summer
its leaves are tarnished,
its fruit beyond reach.
There's an exchange going on
between light, weather,
time and tree in which I'm
a by-stander, asker
of inane questions
in the wrong language.

The tree's rhythm, for
example—bough's rise
and fall—was it learnt
from the sea? Does it mind
that what was orchard
is now city street? Has it
Eden in its genes? Who
is it here for? Balance
and symmetry—imposed or
chosen—seem what it's about,
though the more I look
the less I know. It's
as though some extra sense,
an apple sense, were needed,
a cure for sight's blindness,
an ear for sap, a way
of speaking in blossom.

# *Waiting*

On the dot of eleven-fifteen
I'd phone her. Sunday morning,
after *The Archers*, doing the dutiful
daughter bit. Knew she'd be waiting,
sat with a stack of mags and memories
under her cushion, watching the clock,
the blank telly, the long empty days.

I was glad of the distance. Hated
her waiting—for *him* to come home
to the dried-up dinner; for school
to finish; a night at the pictures;
two weeks in Sidmouth; husbands
for daughters; the doctor's visit;
time to pass, night to end.

Now she's upped sticks and eloped
with the loot of my childhood
and Sunday a.m. finds me fraught
as a homing pigeon thwarted of home.
All's latitude and longitude
And no north pole. No coo. All moan.
And the only voice I hear's my own

from years ago; running behind her
up the street, calling, 'Wait! Wait for me!'

# My Father's Chandelier

It was love at first sight.
He bought the house that housed it.
At night it turned our hall
into the planetarium
or a Viennese ballroom poised
for Strauss waltzes. It was Europe
lighting up its candles,
my father's happy-ever-after
fairy tale. Mid-century my sister
danced her bridal night under it.

We sold it. It was too showy,
too difficult to clean. We had no room
for it and no heart. Now we go
for side lights, lights that cast shadows,
or those cheap, non-lasting paper shades
that shift and shake in the many draughts.

Yet still it shines in memory's dark,
my father's dream, a hanging basket of light,
impossible to put out.

## *International Trader*

Died, only half-way through
the quest to *Waring & Gillow*'s three piece suite
and the crystal chandelier and five-star holiday hotel
in Majorca and the captaincy of the golf club.
Died, saying *There is still so much I want to do.*
Died, with your trilby still set north for treasure,
before I was ready,
before you were ready,
before I'd found another love,
while I was still trawling behind you,
you, the international trader
in that commodity persistence,
who told me to try and try
and try again.
And again.
And then didn't yourself
practise what you preached
but lay felled
by the first blow
flat on your back
with an oxygen mask clamped
on your mouth,
doing what you told me
never to do,

going out,
and slamming the door behind you.

## *Drinking Brandy on Whitstable Beach*

—for Naomi and Tim

As if this is what I was meant for
and it's taken forever to find place
and vocation. I'm swashbuckling, hearty
and fresh from the sea. Over
the sea-honed stones, exultant I crunch
in my old-salt's boots. It's sure
stones, sea's sting and brandy's burn
that I love, sitting and swigging
on a groyne that won't last; facing
the music with a big globed glass
in my gladly cold hand. Happy at last,
drinking brandy on Whitstable beach.

All those childhood years spent
watching the men gargle the strong
stuff and now I've the art
of the fragile goblet, the magic draught:
two fingers either side the stem;
globe in palm; the lingering,
appreciative swirl and sniff before
the first sip, then the fire
in the throat, fierce as a kiss.
O I could make a career out of this,
drinking brandy on Whitstable beach.

# Arkadi Monastery

i

All week your heart's been battered
by the three infinities—mountain
sea and sky—so now you take the bus
out of the roistering town and climb
hill upon hill, through healing olive
groves and up such narrow windings
you wish for a bus of bendable rubber.
A halt, close on some scraggy edge
of eternity has you closing your eyes
while the driver plays bouzouki music
nice and loud and adds hoots (animato)
and smiles in his mirror from which
hangs his insurance—the Virgin Mary,
(in a ring of glass diamonds); a Phaistos
disc; a bright blue eye, primitive and plastic.

ii

And when you arrive at what feels like the top—
only there are more hills, further and beyond—
and the bus goes asthmatically off, you find
yourself high on a hill with its top
like a hard-boiled egg sliced off and it's dusty
and silent and sunny and your heart lifts off
like a plane from the runway. The quietness is such
it's as though your ears were suddenly cleared
of the world. You hear bees in the gorse; see,
among musical goats, a grave-bearded one pacing
precisely along a wall as if telling his beads.

So what you're aware of first of all
is the dusk peach walls, the orange trees,
the light and shade of cloistered walks,

the vines at their windings, a homely log stack,
a mop at a door, the one-armed nun (the tourists'
favourite), a glimpse of a monk tending carnations,
and within the courtyard, the peach's dark kernel,
the church where beeswax candles drip their prayers.
Like Jacob's ladder the bell-rope's graceful drop to earth.

iii

In the musuem the past lies peaceful under glass.
You view the monks' embroidered vestments;
*the toilsome work of Parthenios Koitzas*; read,
in painstaking chronicles, random extracts
about the shortage of bread (up two piastres),
the arrival, in Chania, of four hundred two-masters
from Constantinople; the spread of the plague;
the earthquake they thought was the end of the world.
At his desk the museum attendant sells souvenirs
while with one hand he trails black, lascivious
worry beads over his girl assistant's naked thighs.

iv

The guide book takes you on a different tour—
points out the bullet holes in the refectory door,
the tables and benches gashed by sword;
leads to the gunpowder store and the November night
when the Cretan freedom fighters—
choosing death before surrender to the Turks—
fired at the kegs and blew themselves sky-high.
Distant as myth, these heroes and martyrs
*Who in their transcendent struggle conquered death.*
Even as the terms alarm your post-war nerves

the heart, instinctive, leaps to rampaging desire
for love, belief—an enemy to test you at the limits
of the self. Tourists keep cameras bandaged
to their eyes and you, in self-defence, turn history
to a film show in the head. Scan cannon fire,
rearing horse, pall of smoke, outnumbered Greeks,
Turks breaking down the door. Then the courtyard
carnage and the sound-track's awful noise.
The cast is good. Goat-bearded Abbot Gabriel
whose head they skewered ear to ear and the handsome
Konstantine Giaboudakis whose pistol fired the kegs.

*God's fire* they called the flames that dark
November night Arkadi burned. Is this what passion is?
This two-way charge? The spit on which our hearts
are turned? On shelves more suitable for china
there's a line-up of the heroes' sword-hacked skulls
and a woman's freshly braided, morning coil of hair.

v

You fill your water bottle from the courtyard's tap.
Drink grace. Lie under the trees. Hear the pine cones
popping in the heat and take the bus back down.
The woman who plumps herself beside you on the seat
settles a bag abloom with white carnations on her lap.
She gives you one. All night it scents your room.

From: *Twelve Lilts: Psalms & Responses* | 2003

Translations of P. Hately Waddell's Scots versions of
the Psalms, 1871, coupled with personal responses.

# Psalm 84

*How lovely is the dwelling place of God:*
*happy the birds in their nests, happier still is man,*
*and happiest of all, those who see God in Zion.*


How lovely are the Halls of the Lord!
My life slips away in weary longing
for those fine courts. Body and soul
I cry out for God, for the living God.
Even the sparrow has her wee house
and on Your own altar the swallow
makes a nest to keep her young snug.
How happy they must be who live
in that home of Yours, Lord.
They must all be singing to You.

But happiest of all must be the man
whose strength's in Yourself alone,
who has Your ways in his heart,
who's travelled the dry lands
and found the well-spring, whom even
the dripping rain clothes in blessings,
who from strength to strength journeys on
longing to see God in Zion.

Lord, God of Jacob, listen to my prayer.
You who are our shield, look this way,
look down on the face of Your annointed.
A single day in Your court
is better than a thousand elsewhere.
I'd rather crouch in the doorway of God's house
than be housed in the homes of wrong-doers.

A sun and a shield is the Lord.
He lends us grace and glory

and holds nothing back
from those who live truly.

Happy the man, Lord, who trusts himself to you.

## *Longing*

slipped from God's grasp.

Thistledown light, in flight and panic
it was blown every which way.
It couldn't live without a Word to belong to.
It tried *earth, air, fire, water.*
Earth buried it. Air threw it away.
Fire consumed it. Water drowned it.

Then Longing scattered its seeds
over land and sea. Many took root
in *love* and flourished—after a fashion.
But the stronger seeds chose the word
*home* and rooted deeply in its rich thesaurus.

And these were the seeds of Longing
that gave man dreams
and sent him on journeys
and had him hankering, hankering,
as if home was some place known and lost
which he spent his life trying to remember.

## Psalm Eighty-Eight Blues

Lord, when I'm speechless,
when something—not just sorrow
but under that—a dull, numb, nameless dreich
about the heart I hardly seem to have,
when this afflicts me,
when hope's been cancelled,
when the pilot light of me's put out,
when every reflex and response
has been extinguished,

send word, snowdrop, child, light.

# Psalm 90

(lines 1—10)
*Man's like grass and his days like the tide:*
*he comes and he goes but he cannot bide.*


From one end of time to the other,
You have been our home, Lord.
Before the Highlands were uplifted,
Before you shaped the world,
Long before all this, You were Lord.

Full round You bring us from nothing
To nothing. To You a thousand years
Is but a glance, a ship's watch of the night.

You dunk us in dream
Till we're soft and tender as newly-dug peat,
Moist of a morning, hard-dry by night.
We're felled by Your anger,
Done down by Your wrath.

In the glint of Your glower You set out
Our faults, our well-hidden lusts. We drag
Through our days. Our years wear away
Like the swoon of a song. Seventy's our lot—
Eighty, perhaps to the man with the strength
To stick out the struggle. Just a glimpse we're given
Then quick as a wink we flitter home.

# Sparrow Song

Lord, no doubt I'm but a speck
in the dizzying vastness of your vision,
my giant confusions less to you
than the tweak of a tadpole's tail.
I shiver with insignificance yet bloom
with self-importance. Sometimes

viewing your vast from the lock-up
of my little day, I'm all elation,
star-dust in your wondrous planetarium.
Then I fall, terror-struck as a child
in the dark for whom no-one will come.
Nailed in my skull is that tender nonsense
about your care for every fallen sparrow
that even now, in my three score years
I want to believe and am unable.
Accept this, this wanting.

# Psalm 102

(lines 1—11)
*A prayer for the feckless. When feeling forsaken*
*he tips out his troubles before the Lord*


Lord, let this prayer win its way to you.
Reach down and speak home to me
Here, where my days reek of smoke
Where my hearth-stone's blackened
Where such dread swells through me
My heart's burnt to stubble.
I'm worn to the bone with grief
And keening, am like the curlew
That calls in the wasteland, the owl
In the desert, the sparrow who watches
Alone from the roof top. Day after day
Ill-willers jeer and rant madly against me.
Faced by the rough of Your fury
My breakfast's ashes, my soup is tears,
For You have hoisted me up, dangled
Me down and thrown me aside
So that my days dwindle to shadows
And I wither like grass.

## *Call*

Lord, this is pip-squeak calling.
Even with your infinite technology
I expect your line's busy. Therefore
forgive me my witter, tucked up
as I am in my comfy-comfy
with the telly and all its disasters on.
I expect you've seen. I expect
eternity's in Widescreen.

I hardly like to mention my imaginary
ills, the disturbance in my head,
the way I can't live with you or without.
I run out of usefulness. Grow fat
with anxiety. On a fine morning
I rejoice in your mystery. At night
I listen to your silence, and despair.
Dread whatever end's in store.

Attend, Lord, those in valid agony.
I'm just one of the whingers—
though perhaps, as an aside,
you could help me to age as beech leaves do,
transparent enough to let sunshine through.

# A Low Lilt

*He likes my song,* said the Wind,
*My whoosh and whisper, my fugal voices.*

*He likes my song,* said the Sea,
*My rush and roar, my orchestration.*

*He likes my song,* said the Rain,
*My drip and drum, my timpani.*

*He likes my song,* said the Light,
*My shadow dance, my flamenco and shimmy.*

*He likes my song,* said the Dark,
*For I beat time.*

*My song isn't ready,* said the Man,
*I must keep trying.*

# Psalm 150

*The final Hallelujah, very high and grand,*
*made with all that can dirl and blow.*

Hallelujah! Give praise to God in His holy place,
Give Him praise in the stronghold of heaven.
Praise all His wonders and the might of His makings,

With the toot of the horn, with the lute and the harp,
with the drum and the drone and the dance, give Him praise!
With the strings' delight, with the cymbals' dash,
with the cymbals dirling high, praise Him!

With every breath you take, praise Him.

# The Drummer

though he says he doesn't believe,
when he beats the big drum
and when he sets the high-hat dirling
and the crash cymbal crashing
and the splash cymbal splashing
and the riveted cymbal with the shimmering rattle, rattling
and the finger cymbals chinging
and the clackers clacking
and the tom-toms tomming
and the snare drum snaring—
then a certain trance-like look
comes over his sideways face
as though he's listening in
to that heart-beat rhythm
with which we all begin or
maybe tuning in
to earth's hidden pulse,
either way, he's in time and out
and might well be reaching
a hallelujah experience
or something very like,
like happiness.

From: *Sparks!* | 2005

# A Guide takes Henri Rousseau on a Tour of the Glasshouses of Edinburgh's Royal Botanic Garden

*Colours? You want bright colours?*
Let me show you the Glory Bush. Its flowers
remind me of purple satin. Perhaps you'd prefer
the scarlet Bugler from Java or the coral pink
of the passion flower? Here's everyone's favourite—
the bottle-brush plant, such a jolly ochre. And just look
at the Jade Vine! Peppermint green I'd call that.
See how it dangles its claw-like flowers?

*Tigers have claws too?* Indeed, sir. Let's move on
to the Palm House. *You think you've seen one?*
*Eating an antelope?* Well it is dark and steamy.
We have curly palms, kentia palms, cabbage palms
and this one trying to escape through the ceiling,
is *Sabal bermudana*, the Indian fan, at least
two hundred years old. *Now the antelope's crying?*
Well it's not surprising. Oh! Spot the bananas!
*Monkeys? Eating oranges?* No, sir. Not in our plan.

*You like the exotic?* Well, let's say hello
to the Amazonian lily, the sacred lotus,
and these huge, wild ancestors of the African violet.
*You can see a dark woman playing a flute?*
*And snakes sliding out of the trees? One's draped*
*round her neck?* Best to stay calm, sir.
The lady's often here at dusk—fond of the Garden
I'm told and quite a charmer. Let's slip out quietly.

# *Glenogle Swim Centre, Edinburgh*

Up and down up and down up and down I go **(one)** called here as by a mullah calling me to Health at ungodly hour **(two)** of eight a.m. breaststroking up backstroking down possessed of idée fixe twenty lengths much as the Lord has three **(three)** score years and ten in His or so it's said and is He in the swim no He is not He is above it all **(four)** upping and downing as repeat of breakfast dinner tea and much **(five)** as tomorrow and tomorrow and tomorrow **(six)** creeps on a petty pace though creeping is not what I **(seven)** do sometimes the crawl pretending to be fish arm over ear over arm over ear flip flap of fish-tail feet could be fins **(eight)** nice to have gills monotony they say (who?) can give **(nine)** way to revelation through my goggles I see by glimpses **(ten)** now goggled in Glenogle and ear-plugged too such sensory deprivation and O how I love them **(eleven)** the others distracting me from the tee-hee-hee-deum of the self self self **(twelve)** those swimming in lanes the narrow traps of straight and **(thirteen)** narrow moral horror the old men gossiping **(fast one fourteen)** in the shallows and she who gets on my wick always hogging **(fifteen)** the inside lane in never-get-hair wet cap **(sixteen)** even the the ladies known as *the minesweepers* for swimming three abreast chatty happy as they go and **(seventeen)** turning my up and downing into round **(eighteen)** abouting and Jimmy singing *Come Fly With Me* who is maybe seeking another element though this **(nineteen)** if there were sky above and infinity before and behind and if it were only sea spread vast and deep is mine so sometimes you **(twenty)** have to make do and of course I enjoy it.

## Two Rounds

Though the year is old and dying,
And the world seems lost in pain,
Joy is hidden undiscovered
Waiting to be found again—
To be found again.

Though the earth is locked in coldness
From hard soil new life shall spring,
And the heart that's frosted over
Into love shall break and sing—
Love shall break and sing.

# To An Unborn Grandchild

I picture you curled up in the dark
Knowing only the pulse of blood,
bump of bone and rib, your mother's
heartbeat. Have you all your toes now?
Are your eyelashes in place?

Get your head down. The head
is always troublesome.
After that it's slither and slide,
blood, mucus, love.

Come easily. Come swiftly.
Come with everything right about you.
Come with a wonderful mix of genes
that takes the best from all of us.

The air will be shocking, I know,
but take a deep breath.
Tell us you've arrived. Cry.

From: *Late Love & Other Whodunnits* | 2008

## Reading in Bed

Best bonus of the solitary life,
late hours, the stack beside the bed as good
as a new lover any night. But now
there's all the courtesies to do, of bed-
side lights and sex and sleep and who's the first
to shut up shop. Tonight it's me. Your thrill-
er, *Scorcher*, clearly is. I snuggle in,
conscious that you're close but miles away
(in Florida, to be precise). I lie
and listen as the turn of pages slows
down time. The hush-hush sound your thumb's rub makes
is like the lap of waves that lulls me off,
tucked up in self while you, on night watch, learn
whodunnit, why and when and worlds roll by.

## Why it Took so Long

You were otherwise occupied
and so, in a thistledown way, was I.
Also living in the wrong town
and not done with the lunacies of youth
or the worse ones of middle age.
There were children, of course,
taking priority in energy, money, love,
and books to write and much mellowing
and tenderising of the heart to be done
and all the impedimenta of history,
fantasy, expectation to ditch,
and the fire wall to take down,
and the barbed-wire brambles to snip,
and the breast plate to strip,
and the look-out to drug,
and one's mother to silence,
and one's cover to blow,
and one's heart to risk.

Even so, when my waist was slim
and my hair still brown,
where were you?

## *Application*

O let me be your bidie-in
And keep you close within
As dearest kith and kin
I promise I'd be tidy in
Whatever bed or bunk you're in
I'd never ever drink your gin
I'd be your multi-vitamin
I'd wear my sexy tiger-skin
And play my love-sick mandolin
It cannot be a mortal sin
To be in such a dizzy spin
I'd like to get inside your skin
I'd even be your concubine
I hope you know I'm genuine
O let me be your bidie-in.

## *Fall-out*

While the war went on, the child
sat in a circle of sunlight. The house shook.
Precarious crockery chattered alarm.
The legs went from under the kitchen table.
Something lay dead on the living-room floor.
The clock flew off. O an heirloom! An heirloom!
Everything spilt. And the dish ran away
with the knife and the ring and the cat's nine lives.

The father howled about the house
blowing the fuses, seizing essentials—
a letter, a photo, his old school tie.
The mother was electrified.
Static frizzled her hair. In a circle
of sunlight the child sat, burning, burning.

# About Your New Family

Today, our daughter and yours went shopping in town.
It was a special occasion. Big sister and little sister
who had two pounds forty to spend. I looked after
the dog, kept politely invisible, thought about sisters
and how there's no substitute for a good one.
I pictured them holding hands. Big sister looking back
to herself as little. Little looking forward to herself as big.
This will be their never forgotten adventure.

Ten years and still my bones don't understand
why your daughter isn't also mine. I want to invent
some new, familial title—might-have-been-mum,
mother once removed, mother-in-store.

It being nearly Halloween, your daughter has bought
and lost, glow-in-the-dark fangs, a pair
of front incisors, greenish and costing forty pence.
I'm to buy them again and send them to her.

I could take out my own and send you those.

# *Big Sister's Coming on a Visit*

Clean whole house, polish shoes,
Here's the news—
Big Sister's coming on a visit.

Put on best dress, wait for train,
Pray no rain—
Big Sister's coming on a visit.

Book the taxis, fly the flags,
Hide the fags—
Big Sister's coming on a visit.

Buy up florist, shine the town,
Fetch the crown—
Big Sister's coming on a visit.

Big Sister coming with big big case
Big Sister coming with smiley face
Big Sister coming with big big heart
Big Sister likes playing big big part.

Big Sister coming with little frightened soul
Big Sister nervous as new born foal
Big Sister coming with dodgy knee
Big Sister coming with bravery
Big Sister coming to visit me.

Switch the sun on, banish blues,
Here's the news—
Big Sister's coming on a visit.

## Astanga Poetry

—For my son, Hamish

It is necessary to learn the anatomy
of language, the asanas of speech
until your grammar's so flexible
you can back-bend an image, stand
a simile on its head, sustain
your sutras. Your metaphors may need
adjustment. This can be painful.

A guru is helpful—Pattabi Jois perhaps
or Wm Wordsworth—though you will still
need to find your own way and voice.
Whatever posture/imposture you take up—
warrior, dog, tree, boat, snake—you must
be wholly inside it. About concentration:
this should be light, balanced, alert.
Be humble on your writing pad. Then

there's the breath. The rhythm
of inhalation, exhalation, inspiration,
the tuning in. I've heard the art
compared to the last stage of that
old song and dance, *the hokey cokey*,
when you put your whole self in
then your whole self out. This may
take years of practice. And much sweat.

# At Miss Foulkes Secretarial College

My father sent me there. Typing, he said
was a skill no girl should be without.
*You'll always be able to earn a living.*

We all sat Upright
at our Upright Machines and clacked
in Unison. Miss F played music
as we got the rhythm          going.
We were PERCUSSION. Our platens
    whiiiiiiizzzzzzzed
our bells                         *trilled,*
we were learning the alphabet
all over again in the grownups' order.
Left hand: `a s d f` —finger across    for *g*.
Right hand: colon `l k j`—finger across    for *h*.
    **do not look down**
at the keys. Soon we will graduate
to words. Soon we will tap tap tap
them out fasterandfaster. Miss F times us with her stop.
Watch. So many words a minute so many words a minute
somanywords ... Nobody told us it was the spaces
                 between
that mattered, earning a living, a living,
                               a living in words.

# Seven Blessings

—For Hamish and Anna on the occasion of their marriage

More to share than to possess
Words that refresh
The forgiving caress
The heart undressed.
Grace to cherish
Friendship to nourish
Love to flourish

## Last Post

*i.m. William Scammell*

Bitter bright autumn's come
and nights are drawing sadness in
while you talk of the final test
and Henry James greeting death
with *Ah, the distinguished thing.*

Here's an indignant note
to say you can't go off like this
who've been my constant and my kin
through thick and thin affairs of heart
and pen. How should I bear

the years without the tie-beam
of your light on late into
the watches of the night? No-one
talks books like you or can bat a lyric
high above the nets

of time with one swift serve.
I see the Muses of the Lakes
gather like angels at your gate.
They drift across your van Gogh field
and send, as harbinger,

one small black cat who's come
to keep you company in these
hard times. Dear Bill, false comfort's not
the pill for you. When all's made clear
it's love that most distinguishes us—

and cradles you.

# To W.S. Graham

Here I am talking to you across
all those years ago or none,
catching your voice on the sound
waves or maybe the sea waves.

Ridiculous man! What a way
to live—cadging money, squandering
yourself on drink, scribbling, scribbling,
talking to ghosts in the night. *I am,*
you wrote, *a nervous man, feeling
unloved and greedy and lyrically manic.*
'O come to my arms my beamish boy'.

Back then, in time was now, when
you read your poems in a Scots parlando,
you towed my heart out beyond the safe reaches.

I would like to find some good words
for you. Ones that you'd like
that are not too fancy. Ones
that would help me come clear.

Sidney, there's such a hullabaloo
of poet voices out there that
it's hard to hear oneself speak.
But now here you are again, new
and newly Collected, interrupting
the silence with your wild tap tapping,
trying to speak—as you always did—
*from one aloneness to another*

or all of us alone together.

## Harbours

—for U.A. Fanthorpe and R.V. Bailey


Not that I believe in them
despite all those symbolic *Roget* suggestions—
*refuge, place of safety, making it to port.*

But just set me down anywhere near one
and I'm all boat, furled sails, an outboard motor
in my throat, oil in lieu of blood, nets
instead of veins, oilskins for flesh

and either I can snug up against the harbour wall,
(leaving the sheets to clink musically against the mast)
and climb the iron ladder to where my dog
is barking and dancing a welcome or
I can unwind the rope from its stud, fix my eye
on the narrow opening out to everywhere
and slowly set forth. It's early morning of course,
before the world's awake. You'll hear the phut-phut,
a sea churn, my boots in the cabin.

I want you to know this is an English harbour
born out of Masefield and ferries and the tug
to leave and the pull to come home.

*New Poems*

# *How to Play the Piano*

i

*Adults of small stature or short legs will find it necessary to sit further forward on the chair\**

Come to the instrument with your hands and heart clean
And your nails clipped. Straighten your spine. Remember
That the weight on the note really comes from the feet.
Saying grace would not come amiss. This is an occupation
Much like prayer. You are about to enter someone else's mind.

ii

*The most harmful and dangerous thing for the pianist is to sit down at the piano in a bad mood—the tension in international politics or a slight impoliteness experienced in the tram; the player will already be unable to concentrate.*

Practise alone. Early morning is best preferably in an empty
                                                               studio.
Lift the piano's wing tenderly. *Let the sensations*
*Of the outside world fade away.* Your right hand must know
Exactly what the left is doing. They must do this without you.
*Try with each repetition to penetrate deeper and deeper*
*Into the essence of the piece.* Work as if in a fairy tale
Charged with turning flax into gold. *Four hours divided*
*Into two equal parts is abundantly sufficient.*

iii

*The pianist…is a whole theatrical company in one person.*
*A good musical performance teaches us not only to listen but to live.*

Be consumed. Lost and in perfect control. Imagine
An audience. Possibly God or your teacher's old mother
Who, before an exam, was brought in from the kitchen
Still in her pinny. Play as if she was still there.


\* All italic references from *The Technique of Piano Playing* by Jozsef Gat (Budapest: Corvina, 1958)

## Other Mothers

Sarah's I'd have liked. Elegant,
cultured, a film and art buff,
at ninety taking a glass of champange
as a pick-me-up.

Or Henry's. Nifty stitcher of patchwork quilts,
sender of perfectly chosen post-cards,
knitter of multi-coloured mittens, dedicated
to the art of being useful.

Or maybe Di's. A sea-captain's wife,
sex on stilettos, rosy and risqué,
bobbing up behind her cocktail bar
plump on sherry and joie de vivre.

Ah but there was mine
with her cool upper arms, her wedding band
that could heal a stye and her perpetual question—
*What's the point? What's the point?*

Mother, I'm still asking.

## Father's Doors

He had this habit with any door he met—
Once shut, he'd stand outside and tap three times.
Impossible to know what impulse took
His fingers so. Was it a hex to ward
Off wrong? His own Morse code for peace or did
He simply doubt that any door—however strong
And even as its keeper slotted snug
Within its slot—was properly secure?
One Two Three. Tap Tap Tap—
Like a spirit announcing itself on a ouija board.

*Were you born in a house without doors?*
He'd call if I forgot. And when in winter
A bout of bronchitis kept me in my bed
He'd shyly poke his head around the door
Demanding *What d'you want to catch a cold for?*
As if I'd chosen to. I'd lie and listen—

There he goes. I hear him now. The three taps
In my skull as if he never meant to close a door
But always wanted in.

## Cousins

i

I'm embroiled in Saul Bellow's *Cousins*.
It should be a short and simple story
about one cousin asking another
to write a letter that might save him
from prison. But one cousin leads
to another and another and another until
the world is peopled with cousins
and all of them asking for something—
money, a visit, affection, attention—
or at the very least an acknowledgement
of family connection, thus calling up
guilt, compassion, duty and impinging
on one's own life and one's own wish
to be wholly solitary and selfish
and to blot out the almost unbearable
knowledge of being part of the human race,
mortal and, in a world teeming with cousins,
somebody's.

ii

*Everyone's a displaced person these days.*
—Saul Bellow

Straight out of secretarial college, seventeen
and with a shorthand speed of 120 words per minute
but little else in the way of worldly wisdom,
I get this job in a seedy solicitor's office dealing
mainly in even seedier divorces, the details of which
I touch type on a clangy old Remington suffering
a mix of horror and awful pornographic fascination
at the terrible endings of love. But there

in that dingy office (Dale Street, Liverpool) the solicitor
tubby, pompous and waistcoated—I discover
my long lost cousin, Reuben, newly employed
as the articled clerk. But no sooner have I found him
than he's *vamoosed*, listed as a *missing person*
having walked out of his life and articled clerkdom
to do something wild or wicked—or so we speculate
not wanting to consider breakdown, madness, unbearable
                                                      sorrow.

Then *voila!* In another city, twenty, maybe thirty years
later and long after my own, probably seedy divorce,
I idle through the phone directory and find him again,
not missing but listed. Reuben. Reuben K. So we meet
up for supper and he brings me *The Joys of Yiddish*
by Leo Rosten and I give him something that belonged
to my mother (his aunt) that I can't now remember
because Reuben is my only link to a whole lost family

and a whole lost faith. Perhaps because there's too much
past to share, meetings lapse, contact dwindles to a Christmas
card and an occasional letter. I like seeing his name,
his black ink a kind of proof of *thereness*. And
I fantasize that one day Reuben might be my way
back into family and faith only to learn he's changed
tracks, is off on the Buddhist Path of Enlightenment,
has left me out on a limb, like a missing person.

# The Warning

Even in their twenties they were known
As the old maids—the two sisters
In their barren shop, still in Victorian garb,
Their hair bunned fiercely back in knots,
Their aprons starched, their counter scrubbed.
Their fate yours should you fail to fetch a man.

Hard to know if there was something begrudging
In their souls or if a blight of shyness kept them—
Even as modesty was binned with the ration books—
True only to themselves, their endurance such
To make you hope some late-wandering god would
Jingle their shop door-bell; turn them into trees.

## Wind, Go Easy

—For Kate

On the apple tree at my gate
So that my daughter,
When she arrives, late
As usual, will be
Welcomed
By open arms of blossom.

# *Economy McConomy*

Some used the short form *Mac*
But that was too slap-on-the back manly
For me. The whole name—with its *ons*
And *oms* like people on their knees—
Weighed me down, felt too heavy to carry.
And try as I might, I could never make
The little c and the big C—Miss Humble
And Miss Proud—sit easily together.
For those who couldn't pronounce it,
Mother, with awful Dickensian aptness,
Rhymed it with *economy*. That sank me.

I wanted the sweetness of her maiden name.
*In Yiddish*, she said, *Kesler means Singing Kettle*.
I put it together with the girl I liked best—
*Araminta*—a name half dance half peppermint.
That's who I was aged nine: *Araminta Kesler*,
Making and unmaking myself for the first time.

# Cargo

*i.m. U. A. Fanthorpe*

On the list of things you wanted to do
Before you died—going to the races,
Reading Gibbon's *Decline & Fall*,
Canoeing down the Thames.

Here's the picture: Rosie paddling
In the prow, you in the stern singing,
I fancy, *Can I canoe you down*
*the river* in your mother's fond contralto.

It can't be done, dear. And so,
Although I know you'd prefer
The Thames—river banks,
The story of England drifting past,
Maybe a swan or two—I give you
The Bay of Largo heading out
To the North Sea from the Kingdom of Fife.

For on this perfectly still morning,
While I was thinking of you
And when it was so early only
The herring gulls and oyster-catchers
Were awake, a man in a canoe
The size of an orange cough lozenge
Paddled slowly across what was hardly
An horizon, more like sea and sky
Imitating infinity. I watched him vanish
Into it and thought of that Viking way
With death, when the dead chief's laid
In his boat, his treasures about him
And set forth on the sea.

So here's your canoe, freighted
With Gibbon, the *Racing Post*—
'The Watcher' tipped for the 3.15 at Cheltenham—
A few thrillers, Rosie's paintings of home,
Your best memories, a poem on the go.

# In Praise of the Variscan

A giant's cradle on which my love is laid—
arms bound by a band around his waist—
then slid beneath the camera hidden
in the cradle's hood which is lowered
to scan his head, lifts to shift him back,
lowers and lifts, lowers and lifts
until all the parts of him are done.

On the screen I begin to see his skeleton
outlined by the radioactive tracer they've injected
in his arm. The making of a man. First
head and shoulder blades, then
the lovely alignment of ribs, (all there),
the nautical knotting of the spinal cord,
the wings of the hip bones,
the neat little blob of the bladder.
Breaking the rules, the nurse shows us
the images. The skeleton of my love
multiplied by four. How else but by this Variscan
could I see the beauty of the inner man?

## Lament for my Spiral-bound Reporter's Notebook on Being Told that We are Now Living in a Paperless Society

For this one has a cheery orange cover and a fat band around its
                                                                               belly
For it is possibly my thousandth
For a reporter's notebook has accompanied me through life
For from the age of ten my pocket money was spent on
                                                                   acquiring them
For it was a reporter's notebook that encouraged me to be a
                                                              reporter
For afterwards it was impossible to give them up
For they became indispensable for shopping lists
For addictive lists
For lists of who to marry and who not to marry
For new year resolutions and the plan of a complete novel
For diaries and memos to self and sometimes even letters
For it is easy to tear out a sheet and then remove the stray bits
                                                                  from the spiral
For all this requires is a bent paper clip
For they are intensely bagable
For it is possible to write forwards, turn over and go backwards
For they are amenable and unpretentious and ready for
                                                     anything even a lament

## Caroline Herschel: Her CV

Knitted quantities of cotton stockings.
Slaved as mother's laundry maid and scullion.
Endured smallpox and typhus.
Was rescued by William and taken to England.
Sang solo in the *Messiah*.
Dressed in layers of woollen petticoats.
Spent long winter nights watching the stars.
Sat in a booth under William's forty-foot telescope
With celestial clocks, a lamp, a journal
And a flask of coffee. Kept an observation record.
When William was too busy to stop and eat
Fed him by hand, like a mother bird her fledgling.
Polished the brass of the telescope.
Was given her own. Slept little.
Went to bed at dawn. Wrote home that she was
*Minding the heavens* and *sweeping the sky*.
Played hostess to troops of wise men. Danced
Through the tube of the largest telescope.
Discovered seven new comets. Rode
On horseback to Greenwich to announce
The seventh's arrival. Moved out of the house
When William married. Minded his son.
Minded. Kept *A Book of Work Done*.

Caroline Herschel (1750—1848) German-British astronomer, sister of astronomer Sir William Herschel and the first woman to discover a comet.

# The Romantic Couple: A Fantasy

They ask me the way to the river.
She's from Latin America. There's a century
of flamenco and fiesta in her face. On the corner
of a Scottish street castanets start clacking
in a swirl of petticoats. He's a professor.
His shoulders are bent with the weight
of philosophy. In the cool of a medieval
courtyard he murmurs Cervantes.

They ask me the way to the river
and such a longing comes over me
as if Segovia had picked up my heart
and used it to strum *Humorada*.
*Take me in!* I want to say. *Take me
into your lives. I'm kith, I'm kin!*
I show them the way to the river,
set off in the opposite direction.

O my dear lost loves,
ask me again the way to the river,
the way to anywhere,
the way to the past.

## Lighting Effects

Cousin Lesley's after a new kitchen light—
something bright enough to cook by,
but not as harsh as the old fluorescent.

And so we go to St Peter's, now
transmogrified into *Lutterals Lighting Shop*
and deconsecrated, so they say

though uncertainly we hush our voices
walk on quiet, respectful feet as if
a forgotten believer still knelt in prayer

or a chorister's long amen
reverberated on within the walls.
*Lutterals* have divided the nave into

sheepfolds, pens. Each species of light—
angle-poise, tiffany, chandelier—
has its own chapel. Tall table lamps

obscure the story of the stained glass
window. All that's left to see is
a greying halo and *suffering* stretched

like chewing gum in wriggly white.
Then I'm flashbacked to childhood and
*The Light of the World* bought for sixpence

at a Catholic bazaar. Fear of the dark
kept it pinned on my wall. How bright it is
here in the halogen kingdom of lost light.

## On Falling Out of Love with Bookshops

Without intent,
With only the slightest shift of consciousness,
With a sense of moving out,
Of leaving things behind.

I remember my grandfather
Trying to explain to my mother
As she over-filled his Sunday lunch plate,
How, with age, his appetite had shrunk.

Do I *need* a new book? There are more
At home than I can ever read.
More that I've read and forgotten.
Now consider how often I've wished
To be shot of lust and hunger.

Yet how desolate it feels here
In the middle of Waterstones
With a twenty-five pound token
In my hand and nothing I want to buy.

# Dear Miss Armstrong

It's too late to say sorry
And fifty years too late to return your book,
but I'd like you to know—wherever you are—
that *When We Were Very Young*
set, once and for all, the aesthetic standard
for books, its exterior—dark green board
with a trio of characters (Bo-Peep, the King
who liked butter, John who had great big
waterproof boots on) stamped
in gold on the front—giving as much
delight outside as the poems within.

However I would like to apologise
for scribbling in your book
in a way that now pains me
to look at, and in particular
for scrubbing out Mr Shepard's
charming picture of bears
(the ones that get you if you
stand on the pavement lines
instead of the squares) in
purple wax crayon. I confess
they scared me which is
a poor excuse. But at least
I didn't deface your name
address and telephone number.

Miss Armstrong, all my life
I have endeavoured—with varying results—
to make outward appearances match
inner reality. It is a fool's mission
for rarely do they come together
as nicely as they do in your copy
of *When We Were Very Young*.

I think it might be a lifetime's
work making outer and inner match.
Perhaps it will be easier
when we are six.

# The Greenhouse

Before my father gave her away,
On cold sunny days
My sister shut herself in there
With a bag of apples
And her library book—
An historical romance wrapped
In cellophane sticky as semen.
It was a sun trap in winter.

On the slatted bench
Big terracotta pots of tomatoes
Gave off their particular musty stink,
Fattened and turned from green to red.

# November on Campus

*…it is unwise to read mathematics when your fire is out.*
—James Clerk Maxwell

A team of gardeners arrive to sweep up the leaves,
hoovering them into heaps, an autumn harvest.

Inside Joseph Black's Chemistry School
a Voggenreiter Press lowers its tonnage—
think six elephants—onto a pinhead
of compound they hope to transform.

Over in Engineering, seven descendants
of William Rankine have drawn
murky water from a cattle farm in Oz
and are trying to scrub it clean.

Physics lights up. The tiers of Mathematics
multiply and multiply. A joyous
student jumps on her bike shouting
*I've just got the purest product ever!*

The gardeners carry away truckfuls of colour.

# A Street Incident

And our morning routines on hold
as a fire engine eases down
our narrow street. No smoke.
No fire but we're held at the window—
like all our neighbours—as a ladder zips up
to the roof and a crane's launched after,
arcing into the sky, setting a platform
for two firemen (small as Lego men
in their yellow helmets) who now aloft
peer down one of a row of chimney pots.

First it's a rope dropped down, then
a long-handled instrument that looks
like something you'd use to roast chestnuts on
and eventually—one hour? two?—they push
down a blanket. Smallest fireman leans over
the pot (conjurer and rabbit come to mind)
and hauls out a fluffy white (now black) cat.
We clap and cheer. Fireman acknowledges
his audience with a bow. Cat, safely boxed,

descends. But what was it thinking of,
this daft moggy, spending a night on the tiles
then thinking a chimney pot a new kind
of cat flap? My partner says that long-haired
cats are not as bright as their short-haired
fellows. So a soppy cat this one, and lucky
to live in a country soppy about pets.

We go back to our morning tasks cheered
and loving. *So shines a good deed in a naughty world*
I think, wondering how many it would take
to redeem us, redeem us, redeem us.

## An English Woman Eats a Vegetarian Haggis in a Scottish Hospital

as being one of those things which
never entered my wildest—
and boy, there's been some wildest—
imaginings. And yes, there's *the best
laid schemes* and *the slings and arrows of*
et cetera—but that it should be
not only haggis, but *vegetarian* haggis
and chosen over and against
steak pie, corned beef stovies or a ham
sandwich, is tantamount
to astonishing. *And* chosen while
poorly, as though the national dish—*their*
national dish—might in some way be healing,
as their country has been to me in
my incomer stay of ten years, which is why,
come 2014 I'm going to vote YES
even though the hospital's version
of vegetarian haggis is perfectly inedible.

## Yellow Poppies

Go away for a few days and the garden's ablaze
with them—wild yellow poppies surely taller
than ever this year and spread as if to fill
every gap with a flash of joy. This must have been
happening in secret—the seeding and rooting,
the waiting until no-one's looking then this rising
and shining. Why the garden's enlightened!
*Look how we outshine all that you've grown*
they seem to say. Now to lie among them, eyes
half-closed, is to receive an intravenous dose
of happiness. I'm glad they're not red. Light
on the eyes and the mind they breathe the delight
of complete insignificance. How did they get here,
dressed in their best, guests at a surprise party?

As children, poppies seemed to belong to us.
We'd pry inside the small, soft green sleeves
to find the wrinkled skins—fairy airmail—folded
within. Then summer over, we'd burgle
the seed-box lantern with its screw-top lid
and send a million new poppies out on the wind.
These must be them, our dreams blown in.

# Abigail's Garden

Grows children, chaos and, of course, a sapling
Apple, tiny and daring its very first blossom.
Walk past and a shock of energy's sparked off
As if it's in the grass or maybe fed
On *Miracle Gro*. So it's no matter that
The fence is down, the gate half off—there's
Too much growing going on to give
To everything its due. Here's a sandpit,
Trike, a mini trampoline. Now bluebells
Have landed. No wonder next door's clematis
Is wanting in or that old ginger cat,
Terrified of metamorphosis or worse,
Wants out. She's bagged a patch of common
Sun-warmed pavement and is nodding off.

# *Jacob and the Angel*

—*after Sir Jacob Epstein*

Having puzzled for many months about what
My father was doing, incarcerated
In his dressing room for hours every day,
Just sitting and smoking, dressed only in
His bathrobe and without his specs as though
Clear vision might inhibit thought, it came
To me that my father, like Jacob, was wrestling with
An angel and that begging a blessing was serious work.

Determination, they all said, was father's
Greatest strength. Was it not he who modified
*If at first you don't succeed, try, try again*
By adding several more agains? So that explained
His silent tryst and clinch with the angel. And this
Was why I'd tiptoe in, collect my pence for school
And go. I'm not sure father knew who it was
Without his specs, but at least the angel did.

## The Visit

If we'd recognised them, it might have been different
but just turning up like that, out of the blue,
the two of them looking so scruffy—the old guy
with a face like thunder, the young one a bit simple
in sandals and a cap that had seen better days—
doorstepping us, cadging food and a bed for the night.

Well, you could hardly blame us for feeling put upon.
Frankly, we thought they might have something catching.
I don't think the word *Scroungers* was said out loud
but it was in the air. Anyway, I didn't like the look
in the old guy's eyes when we said we didn't have room
and supper might not stretch. If looks could kill

as we said afterwards. I admit our mood was a bit
begrudging but how many folk are ready to entertain
strangers at the drop of a hat? We sent them on
their way—couldn't help noticing that for a man
who claimed to have walked all day, the young one
was amazingly light on his feet—in the event

the naive old couple down the road took them in
and claimed—would you believe—that they'd had
a wondrous night. We thought they'd never stop
singing the praises of *our amazing guests*. We just
smiled politely. Suspected alzheimers. Why else
add gold pillars to the front of their cottage?

Well, we're moving on. We've never really felt
at home here. The locals keep to themselves
and lately we've noticed that the river is rising.
There's talk of pollution and climate change,
landslides in which houses just fall from the cliff.
Just our luck to be in the wrong place at the wrong time.

## *In the Swim*

Here he comes! Going like the clappers—
no, not the clappers, more like a predatory
sea monster, a skinned whale with glossy,
lard-pale shoulders and a bobbin for a head,
thrusting—yes, that's the word for it, thrusting
through the water, churning up a storm
like there's no-one else in the pool/the world
but him and he's going to do his fifty lengths
come what mayhem and drownings.

He's in my lane. Lane rage is powering my arms
and legs. My feet twitter olympically. My goggles darken.
A spell on his bobbin and his pale whale shoulders!
*Fuck Off!* I shout, joyously in the splashy crashy waves
we're making together, sea monster and small fry.

## *The Cure*

Knowing the doctor can't possibly consider
all my ailments in a ten minute appointment, I pick
just one. On a postcard I list the other six
and give this to her. I feel much better.

# *Kaddish*

Lordy lord, pick up this little troubled Mama of mine,
Swoop her up in your arms as if she were a toddler,
For a toddler she is at heart and I cannot know
                            what wounded her
Or stopped her growing or held her mind in such narrow straits
That it couldn't escape and left her always on the main road
That was not a main road at all but a kind of dead end
When all the off-the-beaten-track places should have led
                            her astray
Into the highways and byways of joy.

Dust the disappointment off her. Shake her up a bit.
But gently. Remove those bifocals through which she never
                            liked
The look of the world and borrow a little of Puck's magic
That she might see deludedly yet properly. And laugh.

Brook no complaints about Your House (or whatever Mansion
You have in mind.) Dress her in your bestest green. Attend
To her heart. Pump it up a little. Have you a piano?
Is Sophie Tucker with you? Introduce them.

Let her feel at home who never truly felt so on earth
Even when the babies came and the money
That bought fitted carpets, a washing machine,
A cheque book of her very own. The holiday in Capri.

Fish her wedding ring out of the ashes
And put it back on. Re-unite her with the husband
If you think this is a good idea.

May she be dumbfounded by love.